SPACE SCIENCE

SCIENCE FOR LOOKING INTO SPACE

Mark Thompson

WAYLAND
www.waylandbooks.co.uk

First published in Great Britain in 2019
by Wayland
Copyright © Hodder and Stoughton, 2019
All rights reserved

Editor: Amy Pimperton
Design and illustration: Collaborate

HB ISBN: 978 1 5263 0847 4
PB ISBN: 978 1 5263 0848 1

Printed and bound in China

Wayland, an imprint of
Hachette Children's Group
Part of Hodder and Stoughton
Carmelite House
50 Victoria Embankment
London EC4Y 0DZ

An Hachette UK Company

www.hachette.co.uk
www.hachettechildrens.co.uk

The website addresses (URLs) included in this book were valid at the time of going to press. However, it is possible that contents or addresses may have changed since the publication of this book. No responsibility for any such changes can be accepted by either the author or the Publisher.

Note: In preparation of this book, all due care has been exercised with regard to the instructions, activities and techniques depicted. The publishers regret that they can accept no liability for any loss or injury sustained. Always get adult supervision and follow manufacturers' advice when using electric and battery-powered appliances.

CONTENTS

STARING into SPACE   4

MEASURE the MOON   6

SEE WHERE THE SUN ... SETS   8

OBSERVE EARTH'S SPIN   10

TELL THE TIME ... WITH SHADOWS   12

BUILD a TELESCOPE   14

OBSERVE the SUN   16

BECOME the LUNAR PHASES   18

HUNT FOR ALIEN WORLDS   20

SEE COLOURS ... WITH A SPECTROSCOPE   22

EXPLORE THE DOPPLER EFFECT   24

CAPTURE STAR TRAILS   26

BUILD an ASTROLABE   28

GLOSSARY   30

FURTHER INFORMATION   31

INDEX   32

STARING INTO SPACE

Just over 400 years ago, a Dutch spectacle-maker called Hans Lippershey (1570–1619) invented the telescope. This ingenious invention uses lenses to make distant objects look bigger.

People had been looking at the night sky for thousands of years before this time, but telescopes suddenly allowed people to learn even more about the objects that they saw, because telescopes reveal details that cannot be seen with the naked eye.

EPIC JOURNEYS

Travelling around the solar system is another really good way to learn about the planets and objects in it, but it takes years for spacecraft to reach most other worlds.

In 1959, *Luna 2* became the first human-made object to land on another world. It took 36 hours for the spacecraft to reach the Moon from Earth. In comparison, it took the *New Horizons* spacecraft (launched in 2006) about nine years to get from Earth to Pluto – a distant dwarf planet.

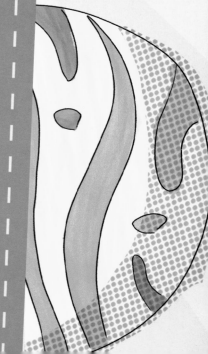

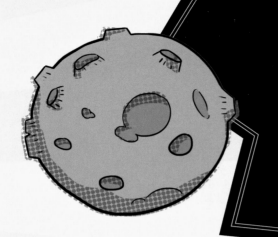

DISTANT GALAXIES

To learn more about objects outside the solar system, we could send spacecraft to learn about them. However, the distances are so great that it would take our fastest rockets hundreds or even thousands of years to reach them.

STARGAZING

Instead of relying on spacecraft, astronomers must use powerful telescopes, such as the Hubble Space Telescope, to examine distant stars, galaxies and gas clouds in detail.

Exploring space with your feet firmly planted on Earth is the focus of this book. There are twelve great activities for budding space scientists, from making your own telescope to studying where the Sun sets, and from learning how to measure the position of stars to exploring how alien worlds are discovered!

MEASURE THE MOON

If you look at the Moon you might see large, flat grey areas (known as lunar maria) and impact craters or you might observe the ever-changing phases of the Moon. It is so far away, and yet it is amazing to think that human beings have actually set foot on the Moon. It took a lot of technology to get there, but we can use a few household items and some very simple maths – called trigonometry – to work out one vital piece of information – the distance to the Moon.

YOU WILL NEED:

- Some modelling clay
- a metre rule or a piece of wood about 1 m long
- a 1-pence coin
- a tape measure (if not using a metre rule)

1 On a clear night when there is a full Moon, put some modelling clay on to the end of the metre rule. Stick the edge of the 1-pence coin upright in the clay.

Look along the rule so that the coin lines up with the Moon.

2 If the coin appears bigger than the Moon, then extend the rule away from you. If the coin appears smaller, then move the rule closer to you.

When the coin covers the Moon perfectly, measure the distance from the coin to the point on the rule where your eye is.

3 Use the sum below to work out what the angular size of the coin is.

$$\text{angular size of coin} = 57.3 \times \frac{\text{diameter of coin (in cm)}}{\text{distance measured in step 2 (in cm)}}$$

4 As you made the coin to appear to be the same size as the Moon in step 2, and you have worked out the angular size of the coin in step 3, you now also know the angular size of the Moon. Work out the Moon's distance from Earth with the sum below.

$$\text{distance to Moon} = 57.3 \times \frac{347{,}500{,}000 \text{ cm (diameter of Moon in cm)}}{\text{angular size of coin (from step 3)}}$$

5 The answer gives you the distance to the Moon in centimetres. To work out what it is in kilometres, divide your answer by 100,000.

6 The average distance to the Moon is 384,400 km. How close to this number is your answer?

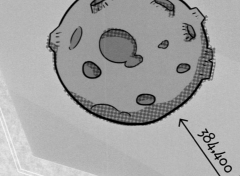

384,400 km

SPACE FACT

Accurate measurements of the distance to the Moon are made by bouncing a laser off the Moon. These measurements have revealed that the Moon is actually moving away from Earth at a speed of 3.8 cm per year.

SEE WHERE THE SUN ... SETS

In which direction does the Sun set? Most people say that it sets in the west. But at some times of the year it sets a bit further north than west (north-west) and at other times of year it sets a bit further south than west (south-west). There are only two days of each year when the Sun sets due west.

Think of a spinning top, it has an almost vertical axis at around 0 degrees. If the spinning top were Earth, the axis around which the Earth spins is tilted at about 23 degrees. It is this tilt that causes the Sun to set in slightly different locations. In this activity you will look closely at where the Sun sets over a few months.

YOU WILL NEED:

- a pencil
- a sheet of paper

1 On a sunny day, wait until sunset (when the Sun is low in the sky). Head outside with your paper and pencil, and an adult you trust.

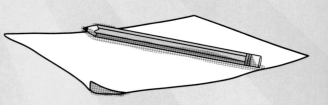

2 Look for the Sun, but DO NOT look straight at it. Find a horizon in the same direction. Sketch the horizon to show where all the main things you can see are. Make a note of where you stood when you made the sketch.

RED ALERT!

You must get an adult to help you and you must follow these instructions carefully. NEVER look directly at the Sun. It can cause blindness or permanently damage your eyesight.

3 When the Sun touches the horizon, draw a circle as accurately as you can to show where the Sun is. Make a note of the date and time next to the Sun.

4 After a few days or even a week, go outside again at sunset with your pencil and the same piece of paper from step 1. Wait for the Sun to touch the horizon and again mark its position, date and time.

5 Repeat this as many times as you can.

6 What do you notice? Early in the year you should see the Sun setting closer to the north-west. In the second half of the year you should see the Sun setting closer to the south-west.

SPACE FACT

On Venus the Sun rises in the west and sets in the east. This is because Venus spins clockwise around its axis, whereas Earth spins anticlockwise.

OBSERVE EARTH'S SPIN

Early astronomers thought that Earth was at the centre of the Universe and that everything orbited around it.* In reality, Earth is not at the centre of everything, it is simply that Earth's rotation around its axis makes it seem like everything else is moving around us.

It takes Earth about 24 hours to complete one rotation, which is why we have 24 hours in a day. If you measure it carefully, it actually takes a little bit less than 24 hours. In this activity we measure the time it takes for the Earth to rotate once.

* see the glossary for a further explanation of this (the geocentric and heliocentric models)

YOU WILL NEED:

- an outside wall of your house
- a piece of chalk
- a stopwatch

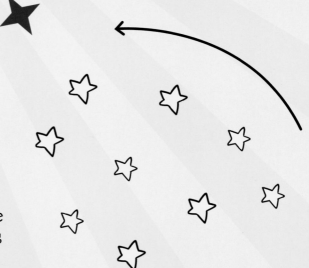

1 On a clear night, watch the stars moving in the sky for an hour or so. Notice which direction they are going. That 'movement' of the stars is actually due to Earth spinning.

2 Make a note of the time. Find an outside wall of your house and chalk a cross on it at head height. Ask permission before you chalk on any walls!

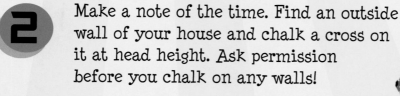

3 Place your head gently against the cross and look along the wall to its edge. Choose a bright star. When it appears to touch the edge of the wall, start your stopwatch.

03.4510

4 Go indoors and put the stopwatch somewhere safe, but leave it running.

5 If the following night is cloudy then you will have to start again on the next clear night. If the following night is clear, take your stopwatch outside about 10 minutes earlier than the time you noted in step 2.

6 Put your head against the cross again. You should see the same star close to the wall. As soon as the star appears to touch the wall, stop your stopwatch. It should show a time a little bit less than 24 hours.

23.5548

The exact time it takes for Earth to spin once on its axis is 23 hours, 56 minutes and 4 seconds. How close to that time did you get?

SCIENCE FACT

Not all planets spin at the same speed. Venus is the slowest planet and takes 243 days to complete one rotation.

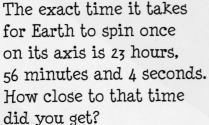

TELL THE TIME ...WITH SHADOWS

We know that Earth takes one day to spin on its axis. This regular and predictable pattern is incredibly useful. Long before clocks and watches were invented to tell the time, people used the Sun to work out the time of day.

Sundials use the movement of the Sun in the sky to cast a shadow, usually from a vertical part called a gnomon on to a flat plate, called a dial. In this activity you will make a sundial with a pencil and a paper plate.

YOU WILL NEED:

- a paper plate
- a ruler
- a pencil
- a protractor
- modelling clay
- a compass

1 Turn the paper plate upside down. Use the ruler to draw a straight line from the centre to the edge. Write the number 12 at the edge.

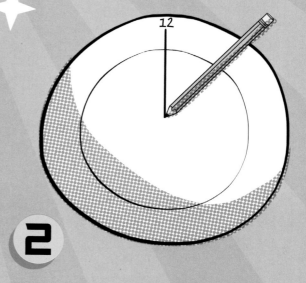

2

Use a protractor to mark off lines around the plate every 15 degrees. Draw seven lines to the left of the number 12 and seven lines to the right. Add the numbers and 'a.m.' and 'p.m.' as shown.

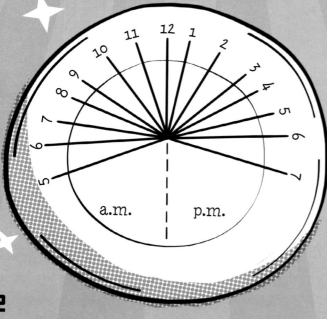

 3 Poke the pencil through the centre of the plate, leaving most of it above the plate as shown. Use the modelling clay to hold the pencil in place if it is a bit wobbly.

4 On a sunny day, take your sundial outside. Use a compass to find north. Place your sundial on a flat surface with number 12 pointing north,

 5 You should be able to read the time from the sundial by looking at where the shadow of the pencil lies.

HISTORY FACT
Stonehenge is an ancient circle of massive stones in Wiltshire, UK. They are thought to have been used along with the position of the Sun to work out what time of year it was.

BUILD A TELESCOPE

Over centuries, astronomers have learned a lot about the Universe. Everything they have observed outside the solar system has been seen through telescopes of many different types and sizes. Refracting telescopes, which use lenses to collect light, were invented first. Reflecting telescopes use mirrors to collect light.

Both of these types of telescope collect light and focus it to make distant objects brighter, clearer and magnified. In this activity you will make a refracting telescope so that you can observe objects in space!

YOU WILL NEED:

- two magnifying glasses (ideally both should be about 5 cm in diameter)
- a newspaper
- a friend or family member
- a ruler
- a long cardboard tube (a wrapping paper tube is perfect)
- a sticky tape

1 Look at the newspaper through one magnifying glass lens. Hold the second lens between your eye and the first lens. Adjust the distance between the lenses until the newsprint looks in sharp focus.

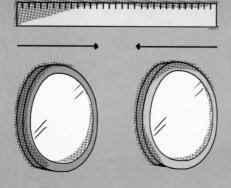

2 Ask your helper to measure the distance between them.

3 Cut a slot in the cardboard tube about 3 cm from one end, but do not cut it all the way through. Slot one of the lenses into it so it sits inside the tube. Hold it in place with sticky tape.

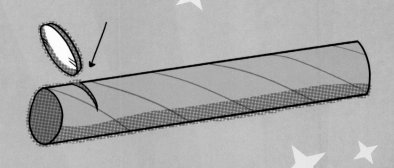

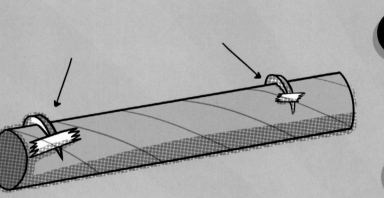

4 Cut another slot in the tube. It should be the same distance from the lens in the tube as the measurement in step 2.

5 Fix the second lens in place with sticky tape. Cut off any extra tube, leaving about 3 cm in front of the lens.

6 Your telescope is finished! All you have to do is go outside and explore the night sky with it!

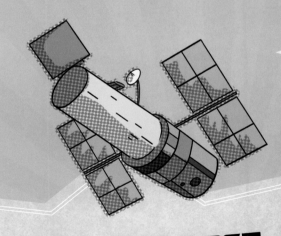

SCIENCE FACT
The Hubble Space Telescope orbits Earth and uses its mirrors to take incredible images of objects in deep space. It took its first picture in May 1990 and is still working today!

OBSERVE THE SUN

The Sun is very important to us and for life on Earth, but the Sun is just an ordinary star among billions of other stars in the Universe. The Sun isn't too big or too small and it's not too hot or too cold. In fact it's pretty average.

The distance between the Sun and Earth varies throughout the year. At its closest, the Sun is 147 million km away. The next nearest star, Proxima Centauri, is 40 million, million, million km away! The Sun emits a lot of light and is very dangerous to look at, but if you are careful and ask an adult to help, then in this activity you can safely observe the Sun.

YOU WILL NEED:

- a pair of binoculars
- two pieces of A4 white card
- scissors

1 On a sunny day, look through the binoculars at a distant tree or building. Focus them so you see a sharp image.

2 Cut a hole in the middle of one piece of card so that it fits over one big lens of the binoculars and blocks the lens on the other side.

DO NOT look through the binoculars during the rest of this activity.

3 Point the large end of the binoculars at the Sun. DO NOT look through them. Look at the shadow it makes on the ground. Carefully adjust where the binoculars are pointing until the shadow is at its smallest.

4 Place the other piece of card about 30 cm away from the smaller end of the binoculars. Adjust the focus ring until you get a bright white disk. If the image is a bit blurry, adjust the focus again to sharpen it.

5 Look at the disk that has been projected on to the card. Can you see tiny black specks? These are called sunspots. You may see lots or hardly any at all.

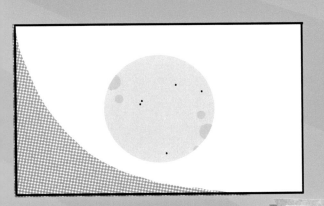

RED ALERT!

You must get an adult to help you and you must follow these instructions carefully. NEVER look directly at the Sun. It can cause blindness or permanently damage your eyesight.

SCIENCE FACT

The Sun is a big ball of gas. The part that you can see during this activity is known as the photosphere and it radiates the light that we see. The word photosphere comes from the ancient Greek words 'photos' (light) and 'sphaira' (sphere).

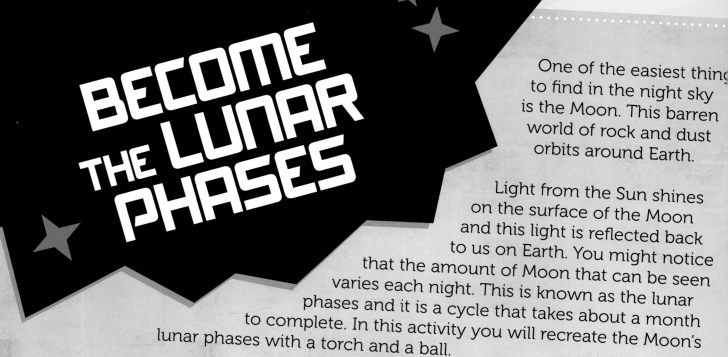

BECOME THE LUNAR PHASES

One of the easiest thing to find in the night sky is the Moon. This barren world of rock and dust orbits around Earth.

Light from the Sun shines on the surface of the Moon and this light is reflected back to us on Earth. You might notice that the amount of Moon that can be seen varies each night. This is known as the lunar phases and it is a cycle that takes about a month to complete. In this activity you will recreate the Moon's lunar phases with a torch and a ball.

YOU WILL NEED:

- a ball – it can be small (tennis ball) or large (football)
- a friend
- a torch

1 Stand in the middle of a dark room with the ball. Ask your friend to turn on the torch.

2 Face your friend and hold the ball at arms length and a little above your head. Ask your friend to shine the torch at the ball (but not in your eyes!). You should see the half of the ball facing you in shadow. This is the New Moon phase where the Moon is between Earth and the Sun.

3 Slowly turn 90 degrees to your left. You should see the right half of the ball lit up and the left half in darkness. This is the First Quarter phase.

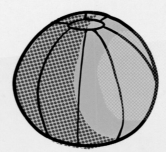

4 Turn another 90 degrees to your left. Your back is towards your friend and the half of the ball facing you should be fully lit up. This is the Full Moon phase.

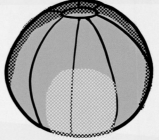

5 Turn another 90 degrees to your left. You should see the left half of the ball lit up and the right half of the ball in darkness. This is the Last Quarter phase.

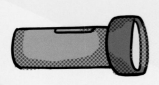
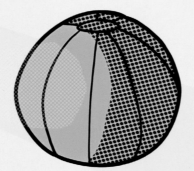

Repeat all the steps, but this time in one smooth circle and watch the phases of the Moon appear and disappear.

LUNAR ECLIPSE

Occasionally, Earth is in a perfect line between the Moon and the Sun. When this happens, the Moon is in the shadow of Earth and we see a lunar eclipse. Turn to the Full Moon position again. Move the ball down a little so that you (Earth) block all the torchlight. You have now made a lunar eclipse!

SPACE FACT

A solar eclipse only occurs during the New Moon phase, when the Moon is in a perfect line between Earth and the Sun, where it briefly blocks light from the Sun during the day.

HUNT FOR ALIEN WORLDS

The eight major planets in the solar system – Mercury, Venus, Earth, Mars, Jupiter, Saturn, Uranus and Neptune – are far away. But they are fairly easy to see because in the vast distances of space they are actually relatively close to us.

Finding planets in other solar systems and galaxies is hard because they are so far away and because planets orbit stars that are much bigger and brighter than they are. If you look at a car's headlights, the glare can make it hard to see anything else. Astronomers use many methods to find alien worlds. One method simply involves blocking out the glare from nearby stars. In this activity you will recreate this method using torches!

YOU WILL NEED:
- two torches (one bigger and brighter than the other)
- a friend
- a few small objects, such as a grape, a coin and a small toy
- a tape measure or ruler
- a large spoon

1 In a dark (not pitch black) room, ask your friend to shine the smaller torch at you, but not directly in your eyes. This torch represents a faint star.

2 Ask your friend to hold a small object close to the torch to represent an alien planet. Can you see what it is? You probably won't be able to because of the glare of the torchlight.

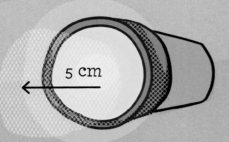

5 cm

3 Ask your friend to slowly move the object away from the torch (sideways) until you can see what it is. Then measure how far away from the torch the object is.

4 Repeat the experiment with the brighter torch to represent a brighter star. You should find that the object has to be even further away from the torch to be seen. The brighter the star, the harder it is for astronomers to find planets.

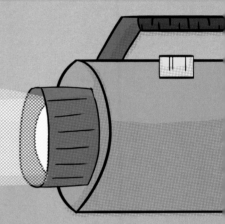

5 Repeat the steps again, but this time close one eye and block out the torchlight with the spoon. This should make any objects close to the torch easier to see.

Astronomers don't use spoons, but they do use this same technique to find distant planets!

SCIENCE FACT

Astronomers have found over 3,000 exoplanets (planets outside the solar system) around distant stars using simple light-blocking methods.

SEE COLOURS ...WITH A SPECTROSCOPE

Astronomers studying objects in deep space often use a tool called a spectroscope. This clever instrument lets scientists carefully study the information inside light.

Visible and invisible light are types of electromagnetic radiation that travel in waves of energy. Studying light with a spectroscope tells us how hot an object is, how far away it is and what it is made of. This can tell scientists a lot about the Universe.

In this activity you will make a spectroscope and use it to look at the spectra produced by different sources of light.

YOU WILL NEED:

- a large box
- a blank CD or an unwanted DVD disc (check that it is OK to use)
- a long cardboard tube
- scissors
- an adult to help you
- two business cards (or pieces of thin card business card size)
- sticky tape
- aluminium foil

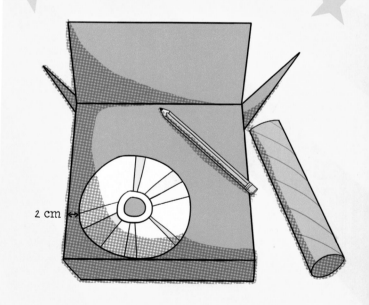

2 cm

1 With the box opening facing away from you, put the CD on the box *exactly* as shown. Draw around the hole in the middle of the CD.

Remove the CD. Put the cardboard tube over the circle and draw around it. Move the tube 2 cm to the right and draw another circle. These two overlapping circles create an oval. Ask an adult to help you cut this out.

2 Turn the box so that the oval is now on the right-hand side. Place the CD *exactly* as shown and draw around the centre circle again. Draw a vertical rectangle 1 cm wide and 4 cm high with its bottom on the bottom edge of the circle. Ask an adult to help you cut this out to make a slit.

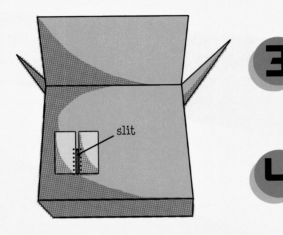

slit

3 Tape both business cards over the slit as shown. The thin gap must be the same width all the way along. This is where light will enter the box.

4 Tape the CD (shiny side up) to the inside, opposite the slit. The left-hand edge of the CD must line up exactly with the slit.

5 Put the cardboard tube in the oval hole. Look through it to be sure it is pointing at the CD. Tape it in place.

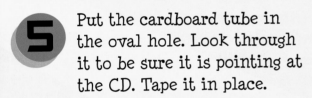

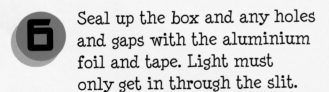

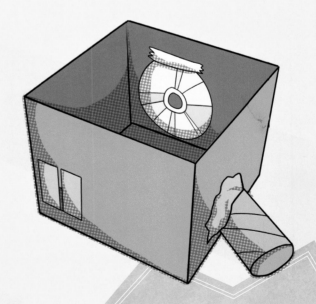

6 Seal up the box and any holes and gaps with the aluminium foil and tape. Light must only get in through the slit.

7 Take your spectroscope into a dark room. Turn on a lamp and point the slit at the light. Look through the tube and you should see a colourful visible light spectrum. Try another source of light, such as a torch, and compare the light spectrums.

SCIENCE FACT

The visible light spectrum contains six main colours: red, orange, yellow, green, blue and violet.

EXPLORE THE DOPPLER EFFECT

The Universe is expanding, which means that most galaxies are moving away from each other. As space expands, the light from galaxies stretches.

Astronomers studying light through a spectroscope (see pages 22–23), see that the stretching causes light to shift towards the red end of the spectrum. This is known as redshift, and it helps space scientists work out how fast a galaxy is moving.

As a galaxy moves away, the light waves spread out behind it. This is called the Doppler effect. When an emergency vehicle drives towards and then away from you, the sound from the siren changes. This is because the sound waves bunch up in front of the vehicle and stretch out behind it. Shorter wavelengths have a higher pitch than longer wavelengths. In this activity you can create your own Doppler effect with a model car.

YOU WILL NEED:

- a sheet of A4 paper
- scissors
- a toy car
- some sticky tape

1 Cut two strips of paper, roughly 2 cm wide, along its longest length.

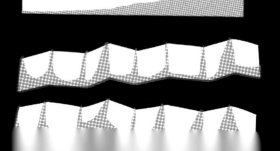

2 Take one strip and make a 1 cm fold at one end. Turn it over and make another 1 cm fold from the same end. Continue until the entire strip of paper is folded into a concertina. Repeat with the other strip of paper.

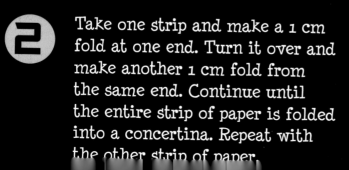

3 Tape one strip to the front and the other strip to the rear of the car.

4 Tape the other ends of the strips to the top of a table. Neither strip should be tightly bunched up nor stretched out.

5 Move the car forwards and backwards to simulate the Doppler effect. As the car moves toward you, the folds in the front strip bunch up.

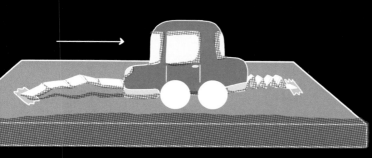

This represents light (or sound) waves heading towards you. They have a shorter distance to travel, so the wavelengths are closer together.

When the car moves away from you, the folds stretch out, simulating redshift. Light or sound waves moving away from you have further to travel, so the wavelengths are further apart.

SPACE FACT

The redshift caused by the galaxies moving away from us tells astronomers that 13.7 billion years ago they were all in the same place when the Universe appeared in an event called the Big Bang.

CAPTURE STAR TRAILS

As you read on pages 10–11, the movement of objects across the sky is caused by the spin or rotation of Earth around its axis.

If you stand and watch for long enough you can see the apparent movement of the stars. An easier way to see this is by photographing the stars to capture their star trails. If a camera is set up on a tripod to keep it steady and left pointing in one direction for a period of time, then, as the Earth spins, the camera will move with it to point at different parts of the night sky.

YOU WILL NEED:

- a DSLR camera on a tripod (DSLR stands for Digital Single Lens Reflex)
- a piece of card

1 On a clear, moonless night and with an adult you trust, set up the DSLR camera on its tripod outside. Point the camera lens up to the sky.

2 Look on the camera lens for the infinity symbol ∞ (it looks like a number 8 on its side). Twist the camera focus ring until it lines up with the ∞.

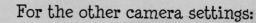

3 For the other camera settings:
• set the ISO to 400
• set the aperture as wide as it can go
• set the exposure to the longest timed setting (probably around 20 or 30 minutes).

(You might need an adult to help you with these settings.)

 That's the hard bit done! Place the piece of card in front of the camera lens and press the shutter button to open the shutter. Count to five and then remove the card.

If you want to, you can go indoors while the camera takes the picture. Or you could stay outside and look at the stars!

 After the time is up, go outside and look at your picture. You should see a dark sky and the stars trails as curved lines on the picture. If the lines are a bit fuzzy, change the focus a little and try again.

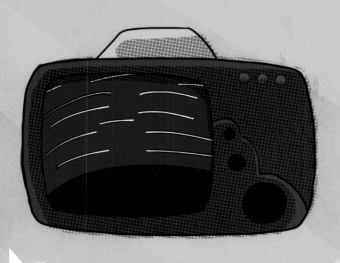

SCIENCE FACT

Even short exposures can capture stars trails. The stars trail because Earth is spinning and the camera is sitting on Earth.

BUILD AN ASTROLABE

An astrolabe is an instrument used by early astronomers. The first ones were made of brass and wood and were used to work out the time of day and the length of day.

If an astronomer knew how high the Sun or stars were in the sky, they could also work out where they were on Earth! This very important instrument was used by astronomers to find their way around, long before sat nav was invented! For this activity you will make your own astrolabe to measure the height of stars in the sky.

YOU WILL NEED:

- some cotton thread
- a ruler
- scissors
- a protractor
- a washer or nut
- sticky tape
- a straw

1 Cut the cotton thread to a length of about 20 cm (so it is a little bit longer than the radius of the protractor).

2 Tie the washer or nut to one end of the thread. Tape the thread to the middle of the straight edge of the protractor. The end with the washer should hang down below the curved edge of the protractor at exactly 90 degrees.

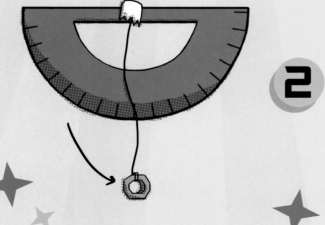

3 Tape the straw along the straight edge of the protractor. Make sure that it is not in the way of the string.

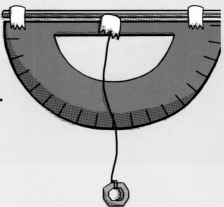

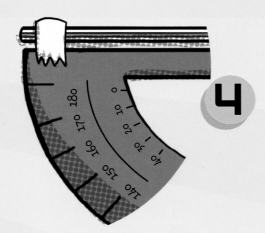

4 Notice that there are two sets of numbers around the protractor. Look at the numbers around the *outside* edge. Find the end of the straw closest to the number 180. This is the end that you will look through.

5 Pick a star in the night sky. Look at it through the straw and read the number of degrees on the outside scale that the cotton marker crosses.

6 You should have a number higher than 90. Subtract 90 from that number and this will give you the angle of the star's height above the horizon.

For example:
130 degrees - 90 degrees
= 40 degrees.

SCIENCE FACT

Measuring the height of stars in the sky is a technique used today by spacecraft to find their way around the solar system.

GLOSSARY

ASTROLABE an instrument used to measure the height of objects in the night sky and to measure latitude – the distance of a place from the Equator

AXIS an imaginary line around which something rotates

BARREN a place with no trees, plants or other life

BIG BANG the event that marks the beginning of the Universe

CRATER a dent in a planet or moon's surface caused by an object crashing into it

DWARF PLANET a large rounded body in space with its own gravity, but which is not big enough to be classed as a planet

ELECTROMAGNETIC RADIATION the flow of energy in the form of waves, such as light waves, X-rays and gamma rays

EXOPLANET a planet that orbits another star

EXPAND to get bigger

GAS one of the three main states of matter. A gas can expand, squeeze, and flow from one place to another.

GEOCENTRIC a model of the Universe with Earth at the centre, which astronomers used until about the late 16th century

HELIOCENTRIC a model of the Universe with the Sun at the centre, devised by the astronomer and mathematician, Nicolaus Copernicus, in the late 16th century

HORIZON where Earth's surface and the sky appear to meet

INFINITY a symbol used for something too big to be counted

LASER an intense beam of light

LENS a specially curved piece of glass that is used to focus light, often used inside a telescope

MOON a natural satellite that orbits a planet

ORBIT a circular or oval path one object follows around another

PHOTOSPHERE the visible surface of the Sun

SOLAR ECLIPSE an event when the Moon is directly between the Sun and Earth, and the Moon obscures the Sun for a short time

SOLAR SYSTEM the planets, moons and other space objects that orbit the Sun

SPECTRUM a range of things, such as the range of colours in the visible light spectrum

SUNSPOT gas spots on the Sun's surface that look dark compared to the rest of the surface

TRIGONOMETRY the branch of mathematics that deals with triangles and angles

UNIVERSE space and everything it contains

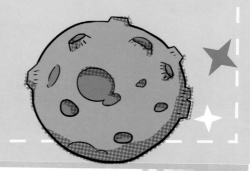

FURTHER INFORMATION

BOOKS

Astronomy for Kids: How to explore space with binoculars, a telescope, or just your eyes! by Bruce Betts (Rockridge Press, 2018)
A Child's Introduction to the Night Sky by Michael Driscoll (Black Dog Books, 2011)
Watch This Space: Astronomy, Astronauts and Space Exploration by Clive Gifford (Wayland, 2016)

PLACES TO VISIT

National Space Centre, Leicester
Royal Observatory, Edinburgh
Royal Observatory, Greenwich London
Science Museum, London

WEBSITES

The Kids Astronomy website has loads of interactive
space activities for budding stargazers.
www.kidsastronomy.com

Astronomy has loads of information about objects you can see in the night sky.
www.astronomy.com/observing/astro-for-kids

Planets for Kids is a great website for exploring the planets in the Solar System.
www.planetsforkids.org

INDEX

astrolabe 28-29, 30
astronomers 5, 10, 14, 20, 21, 22
   24, 25, 28
axis 8, 9, 10, 11, 12, 26, 30

Big Bang 25, 30

clocks 12

day (length) 10, 11
Doppler effect 24
dwarf planet 4, 30

electromagnetic radiation 22, 30
exoplanets 21

galaxies 5, 20, 24, 25
geocentric 10, 30

heliocentric 10, 30
horizon 8, 9, 29, 30

lenses 4, 15, 15, 16, 27, 30
Lippershey, Hans 4
lunar maria 6
lunar eclipses 19

Moon 4, 6, 7, 18, 19, 30

photosphere 17, 30
planets 4, 11, 20, 21
Venus 9, 11, 20
Pluto 4
Proxima Centuri 16

redshift 24, 25
rotation 10, 11, 26

scientists 5, 22, 24
solar eclipse 20, 30
solar system 4, 5, 14, 20, 21,
   29, 30
spacecraft 4, 5, 29
Luna 2 4
New Horizons 4

spectroscope 22-23, 24
spectrum 23, 24, 30
stars 5, 10, 16, 20, 21, 26, 27,
   28, 29
Stonehenge 13
Sun 5, 8, 9, 12, 13, 16, 17, 18,
   19, 28
sundial 12
sunspots 17, 30

telescope 4, 5, 14, 15
Hubble Space Telescope 5, 15

Universe 10, 14, 16, 22, 24,
   25, 30

SPACE SCIENCE

TITLES IN THIS SERIES

Born in Norfolk, author **MARK THOMPSON** has had a fascination with all things in the sky ever since he was a small boy. At the age of 10 he got his first view through a telescope; Saturn in all its glory. It ignited a passion that has stayed with him ever since.

Mark has inspired millions of viewers to get out and enjoy the night sky through his role as presenter on the RTS nominated show *BBC Stargazing Live*. His passion for reaching out to a new audience has found him working on *The One Show*, *This Morning*, Channel 4 documentaries and ITV's prime time breakfast show, *Good Morning*. He is also a regular face on *BBC Breakfast*, *Five News* and a regular voice on *Radio Five Live*.

SCIENCE FOR EXPLORING OUTER SPACE

Out of This World
Hunt for Meteorites
Erupt a Martian Volcano!
Smash into the Moon
'Talk' like a Computer
Freeze a Comet
Create Gravity ... in a Bucket!

Bend Water ... with a Comb
Explore Venus's Atmosphere
Make a Fruit Solar System
Whip Up a Storm ... in a Bottle
Find the Speed of Light ... with Cheese!
Supercool Water

SCIENCE FOR LOOKING INTO SPACE

Staring into Space
Measure the Moon
See Where the Sun ... Sets
Observe Earth's Spin
Tell the Time ... with Shadows
Build a Telescope
Observe the Sun

Become the Lunar Phases
Hunt for Alien Worlds
See Colours ... with a Spectroscope
Explore the Doppler Effect
Capture Star Trails
Build an Astrolabe

SCIENCE FOR ROCKETING INTO SPACE

Reach for the Stars
Escape Gravity
Overcome Inertia ... with an egg
Explore Epic Exothermic Eruptions
Balloon to the Moon
Lower the Centre of Gravity
Blast Off ... with a Chemical Reaction

Launch a Straw Rocket ... with Puff Power
Hurtle to Earth on an 'Eggciting' Mission
Send a Rocket into Orbit
Make Water Weightless
Become a Rocket Booster
Launch the Ultimate Rocket!

SCIENCE FOR SURVIVING IN SPACE

A Dangerous Place
Pack a Space Bag
Inflate a Balloon ... with Microbes
Eat Like an Astronaut
Warm Up with Insulation
Shield Yourself from Meteoroids
Grow Food in Space

Draw a Magnetic Force Field
Make a Biosphere ... in a Jar!
Make Dirty Water Clean (ish!)
Make Your Own Blood
Create Floating Blobs of Water
Cook Toast in a Solar Oven